YOUNG SCIENTISTS INVESTIGATE

Forces and Movement

This edition first published by
Evans Brothers Limited
2A Portman Mansions
Chiltern St
London W1U 6NR

Reprinted 2007

ISBN 0 237 53018 X

British Library Cataloguing in Publication Data
A catalogue record for this book is available from the British Library.

Printed in China by Midas International Ltd

Acknowledgements
Editorial: Su Swallow
Design: Neil Sayer/Rob Walster
Production: Jenny Mulvanny
Commissioned photography: Alan Towse
Copyright © Evans Brothers Limited 1997. First published 1997.

The publishers would like to thank Mr McBride, the staff, parents and children
of Much Woolton JMI School for their help in the preparation of this book. We
would also like to thank the children of Woolton Infant School who appear on
the cover of this book.

For permission to reproduce copyright material the authors and publishers
gratefully acknowledge the following:
Page 6 Alan Towse **page 10** Action Plus **page 14** Stewart Clarke, Action-Plus
Photographic **page 16** Bennett-Dean, Eye Ubiquitous **page 18** Robert Harding
Picture Library **page 20** Colin Jarman, Action-Plus Photographic **page 22**
Robert Harding Picture Library **page 24** Robert Harding Picture Library **page
26** Mehau Kulyk and Victor de Schwanberg/Science Photo Library **page 28**
Robert Harding Picture Library

VISIT OUR WEBSITE
www.evansbooks.co.uk
Evans

YOUNG SCIENTISTS INVESTIGATE

Forces and Movement

**Malcolm Dixon
and Karen Smith**

Evans

Evans Brothers Limited

NOTES FOR TEACHERS AND PARENTS

Pushes and pulls (pages 6-7)
Develop the idea that pushes and pulls cause movement. Make a collection of toys and discuss how each can be moved. Collect photographs of things being moved by pushes and pulls. Talk about pushes and pulls during physical education lessons. Use the word 'force' in your discussion.

Squashing and stretching (pages 8-9)
In discussing the idea that forces can change the shape or size of objects you might demonstrate with an inflated balloon, tube of toothpaste or even a twig.

Gravity is everywhere (pages 10-11)
Use a ball, crumpled paper and other objects to demonstrate and discuss the pull of gravity. Look at the photograph and talk about the pull of gravity on the diver. The marble dropped from the greater height pushes deeper into the sand because it exerts a greater force (push).

Magnets pull and push (pages 12-13)
If possible allow children to use a magnet to pick up a range of objects, including pins. Using strong magnets allow children to experience the 'magic' of invisible magnetic forces.

Friction (pages 14-15)
Try to examine a range of shoes, including trainers, and talk about which surfaces grip best. Can the children devise a way of testing them? Rough surfaces resist movement more than smooth surfaces. Talk about moving easily down the smooth surface of a slide. Ask them to rub the surfaces of their hands together. Friction makes their palms feel hot.

Making things move (pages 16-17)
Collect photographs of bicycles, motorbikes, cars and other vehicles. Talk about how wheels enable movement across different surfaces.

Air pushes (pages 18-19)
Try to emphasise that air is 'real' even though it is invisible. Look at photographs of birds in flight and talk about their streamlined shapes. Relate this to the paper aeroplanes that the children make.

Wind force (pages 20-21)
Look at photographs showing the force of the wind and let the children talk about their experiences. Collect a variety of small objects. Can the children move some of them by blowing? If possible, visit a windmill. Show the children photographs of older and modern windmills.

Slowing down (pages 22-23)
When testing the parachute it is important to consider safety factors. You may find it appropriate to throw the parachute high in the air and watch it open and float to the ground. Gravity pulls the parachute to the ground and the air tries to resist this force, so slowing down the descent.

Water pushes (pages 24-25)
Use the plastic sheet to protect the desks/tables from any water spillage. If the plasticine ball is made into a boat shape, with thin sides and base, it will float.

Levers (pages 26-27)
Other levers that can be found at home include garden tools, wheelbarrows, pliers and crowbars. You might demonstrate how a tin of paint can be opened using a lever. Visit a playground and show how a see-saw is a lever.

Powerful forces (pages 28-29)
Children may be able to observe powerful machines within their neighbourhood such as cement mixers, cranes and the vehicles used to remove rubbish.

Contents

Pushes and pulls

All around you things are moving. They move because of forces. Pushes and pulls are forces. This roundabout is moving because it has been pushed. How could the girl make the roundabout go faster? How could she slow it down?

Nothing begins to move unless a force starts it.

Work with a friend

Join hands and push against each other. Can one person push harder than the other? What happens? Can you pull against each other?

 ### Find out more!

Do you have any toys that need pushes or pulls to make them move? What other pushes and pulls can you find around you?

Make a list of 10 things that use pushes to make them move.

Make a list of 10 things that use pulls to make them move.

Squashing and stretching

Sometimes when you push or pull something it does not move. In the photograph the ball is being squeezed. Pushing has changed the shape of the ball. When you pull an elastic band it gets longer and may break.

What happens to a lump of clay when you push and pull it with your fingers?

Can you think of other things that change shape or size because of pushes and pulls?

Investigate stretching

You will need:
plastic cup
elastic bands
paperclip
felt-tip pen
sand

Ask an adult to fix the paperclip through the top of the plastic cup. Use the pen to make two marks on a thin elastic band.

Fix the elastic band to the paperclip. Put sand into the cup and watch how the elastic stretches. Look at the gap between the pen marks. Does the same thing happen when you use a thicker elastic band ? What happens to the elastic when you empty the sand from the cup?
Try this investigation with a small spring.

Gravity is everywhere

If you throw a ball into the air, it falls back to the ground. Crumple up a piece of paper and throw it into the air. What happens?

Things fall to the ground because they are pulled towards the Earth by a force called gravity. When you jump, run, swim or stand still your body is pulled by gravity.

Gravity pulls everything downwards towards the Earth.

Investigate the pull of gravity

Place the sand in a tray on the floor.
Smooth the sand to make a flat surface.
Drop a marble from waist height into the sand.
What happens to the sand?

What happens when you drop the marble from a greater height?
Why do you think this happens?

Magnets pull and push

If you spill some pins they can quickly be picked up using a magnet. The magnet pulls the pins towards it. This magnetic force is invisible. A magnet will not pull things made of wood, plastic and some other materials towards it.
When two magnets are placed together they either push apart or pull together.

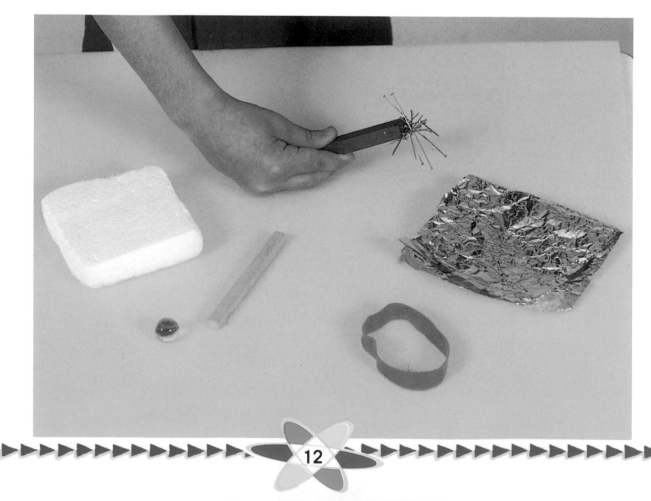

Watch the force of magnets

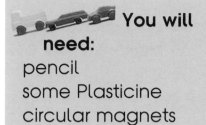 **You will need:**
pencil
some Plasticine
circular magnets

Push the pencil into the Plasticine.
Place one circular magnet over the pencil.
Can you place the other magnets on the pencil so that they 'float' in the air?
Push them down.
What happens when you let go?
Scientists say that the magnets repel each other.

Can you arrange the magnets so that they attract each other?

Friction

Push a book across the top of a table. What happens? The book slows down and stops. This happens because of a force called friction. Friction occurs whenever two surfaces rub against each other. Friction is an important force. Without it wheels on cars and bicycles would not grip on road surfaces.

Look at a your shoes. How do they use friction to grip the ground?

Investigate friction

Use a smooth piece of wood
to make a steep slope.
Let the toy cars roll down
the slope.
Now cover the slope with carpet.
Will the cars move faster, slower
or the same as on the smooth surface?
Test them. What do you notice?
What is the reason for this?
Will the same thing happen with a more
gentle slope?

Making things move

If you need to move something you could drag it. But the force of friction makes things difficult to drag. Friction slows down the movement. If a heavy object is put on rollers there is less friction and the object can be moved easily. Wheels are like rollers. Wheels make it easy to move heavy things. Look at the photograph. The wheels on the lorry make it easier to move the heavy load.

Use rollers to move a brick

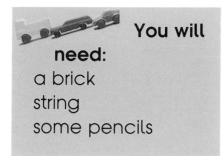

You will need:
a brick
string
some pencils

Fix some string to the brick and try to drag it across a surface. Is it difficult to move? What is the name of the force that is slowing it down?

Now place the brick on a row of pencils. Pull the string. Does the brick move more easily on these rollers?
Can you explain this?

Air pushes

You cannot feel it or see it but air is all around you. When anything moves, the air is like an 'invisible wall' pushing back and trying to slow it down. The photograph shows an aeroplane moving through the air. Look at its smooth shape which lets it cut through the air. We say that it is streamlined.

Look for cars which have streamlined shapes.

Testing air pushes

Find a large sheet of cardboard.
Run with the cardboard held
in front of you.
Does something seem to
hold you back?
What is it?
What happens
when you use
an even
bigger
piece of
card?

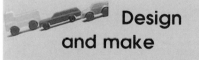
Design and make

Make some paper
aeroplanes.
Try different designs.
Which flies the
furthest?
Can you say why it
flies so far?

Wind force

Sometimes when you are walking on a windy day you can feel the pushing and pulling of the wind. Have you seen leaves being moved along the ground by the wind? The force of the wind can be strong enough to push over houses and overturn cars. In the photograph wind is making the boat move across the sea. Can you think of any other ways we use the force of the wind?

Make a land yacht

Make four holes in the sides of the box. Push two lengths of rod through the holes. The rods must turn easily.
Fix the plates to the ends of the rods.
Try out your yacht. Push it. Does it roll easily?

Use rod and card to fix a sail to the yacht. Test your yacht outside in a gentle breeze. Does the wind push the yacht along the ground? What happens if you use a bigger sail?

You will need:

a cardboard box
2 equal lengths of
  dowel rod
polystyrene or
  paper plates
card
glue
scissors

Slowing down

This man is using air to slow him down. He has jumped from an aeroplane high in the sky and is pulled towards the ground by the force of gravity. When his parachute opens air is trapped underneath it and slows him down.
His parachute lets him float gently and safely to the ground.

Make a parachute

Cut a large square of plastic.
Tie the four lengths of string to the corners of the plastic.
Tie the other ends of the string to your plastic figure.
Roll your parachute and figure into a ball.
Throw them high into the air.
Watch how the parachute opens and floats gently to the ground.
What force is pulling it towards the ground ?
What is slowing it down?

Make parachutes of different sizes. Does the size of the parachute change the way it falls to the ground?

You will need:
plastic bag
plastic model figure
string
scissors.

Water pushes

Large ships like this move across the seas of the world carrying passengers and heavy loads. The weight of a ship pushes down into the water. The water pushes up. The force of the water pushing up is called upthrust.

When you are floating in a swimming pool the water is pushing up on your body.

Feel water pushing

Fill the tank with water. Blow up the balloon.
Place it on the surface of the water. Push the balloon under the water.
Can you feel the water pushing back?
What do you notice about the level of the water as you push down on the balloon?

Try to push other objects under the water.
Can you feel the push of the water on all of them?

Can you make the Plasticine into a shape that floats?

You will need:
plastic tank
balloon
sheet of polystyrene
some balls of
  different sizes
sponge
plastic containers
ball of Plasticine

Levers

Levers are simple machines which help us to do things more easily. A lever can turn a small push into a big force. A small push on a spanner can help to turn a large nut. A small push on a pair of scissors can cut through thick material. Can you think of any other kinds of levers that are used in your home or in your garden?

Have fun with levers

Draw the shape of an animal with a large jaw, such as an alligator.
Use the scissors to cut out the shape.
Draw and cut out a lower jaw for your animal.
Fix the lower jaw to the rest of the animal with a brass fastener.

Look at the photograph. See how the jaw can move. Can you make your model move in this way?

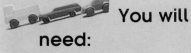

You will need:
card
brass fastener
scissors
felt-tip pens

Powerful forces

When people are building houses, roads and bridges many things have to be moved. Some of these things need really big pushes and pulls to move them. Often machines are used. Look at the machine in the photograph. It is a bulldozer and it uses powerful forces to move soil and rocks. Look out for other machines. What are they used for?

Make a model bulldozer

Make four holes in the sides of the larger box. Push two lengths of rod through the holes. Make sure they turn easily. Use glue to fix cotton reels to each end of the rods. Cut corrugated card to make tracks to put around the cotton reels. Glue the smaller box to the top of the larger box. Use card to make the front pushing part of the bulldozer.

Push your model.
Does it move
easily?
Can it push
things out of
its way?

Index